Finding Peace
at the
Center of the Storm

Finding Peace
at the
Center of the Storm

You Can Quote Me

Nancy Ganz

LUMIERE PUBLISHING
2018

Cover design: Michelle Baron
Illustration and design: Michelle Baron
pages: 33, 54, 74, 83, 116, 131

ISBN 978-0-9993772-0-8

Library of Congress Control Number: 2018906140

All Illustrations used under registration agreement
Printed in the Unites States of America
First Published 2018

LUMIERE PUBLISHING
_____

lumierepublishing.net
Newton, MA

Thank you for purchasing this book through the publisher
and approved outlets.

In celebration of you

From the first moment we burst into the world,
we occupy an important place in this global tapestry.
With multitudes occupying the same plane,
how do we find peace at the center of the storm?
Find harmony in the cacophony? Avoid the draw of
a negative maelstrom threatening to pull us into a
swirling abyss? A simple compact with ourselves
can guide us to a life well lived, with our destiny
designed by our thoughts and actions.

Feel and Express Love

Seek and Speak Truth

Create with Your Thoughts

Take Full Responsibility for Yourself and Your Life

Treat Others with Grace and Respect

*I*n the darkest cave,
one candle can light the way.

⇀ 2 ↽

$\mathcal{F}$ree yourself from others' beliefs
about who you are.

The road to integrity is as wide as your own two feet — there is no almost.

↣ 4 ↢

*W*hen life's pressures feel crushing, remember...

*C*oal, put under pressure, either crumbles
or becomes a diamond.
So too with us.

$\mathcal{T}$ime drifts by without hellos or goodbyes

It enters without question and parts in disguise

I'm always fooled by Time's tricks of the trade

For it is the Master, myself just a slave

Change is inevitable — the world
turns everyday.

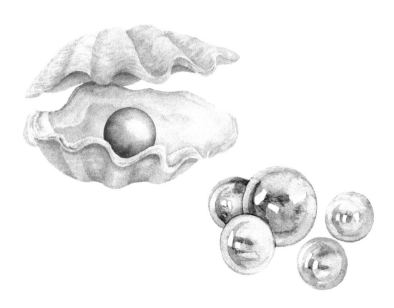

$\rightharpoonup$ 7 $\leftharpoondown$

*E*verything does not happen for a reason,
but we can make reason out of
what happened.

*L*eadership by its very definition means
standing out front alone —
not choosing comfort in a crowd.

A baby bird must open its mouth to receive a worm. So too, you must open your heart to receive love.

The only way to get out of the spin cycle of regret is to turn off the machine.

$\mathcal{E}$xpectations are the ruination of life.

Go for everything.
Expect nothing.

*I*n the garden of life,
focus on the flowers and foliage
instead of the dirt.

*I*f you want the universe to catch your dreams…

you have to throw the ball.

$\mathcal{T}$oday is the Tomorrow you Dreamed of Yesterday

✥ 15 ✥

*P*ast is past.
It doesn't have to be prologue.

$\mathcal{M}$ind your P's and Q's,
Not your B.S.'s.

*W*hatever hand you were dealt —
Play your high cards!

$\mathcal{L}$ife is like an unending movie.
Each of us enters and exits at different
points in the plotline.

$\mathcal{I}$f someone is consistently and continuously
unkind, unclear, and unsupportive, then
there is no place for that person
in your movie.

$\mathcal{Y}$ou are the
producer,
director,
and actor
in your life's play.

$\mathcal{W}$rite yourself in as the lead.

$\mathcal{H}$ave the courage to be different —
you are anyway.

*D*ream big
Aim high
Trust your heart

Live life with no regrets: Say Yes

Things, people, places, and experiences are only foreign because they aren't familiar.

Once they are familiar,
they are no longer foreign.

LIVE LARGE — and barriers will vanish.

"*I* should..." means: DO it.

"*I* should have..." means: Lesson Learned.
No need to berate yourself for not
having the wisdom before.
Let it go.

When pursuing your dreams,

— "No" —

just means find another way.

*I*t is natural to resist change,
but futile to do so.

Like a flashing circuit board, numerous
options light up for us every minute.

Entrenched patterns and a reflexive instinct
to protect your identity can sideline freewill
by preselecting the choices you make.

Release the past.
Take charge of your choices.

People don't become bitter because they are wrong. They become bitter because they are right and have been wronged.

Better to tell yourself out loud that you are "right" and then move on.

*T*ears flowing from grief are like rain
to the roots of a tree.

*I*f you can think it — you can do it.

$\mathcal{T}$omorrow is only a dream away.

Life is too short to carry the burden
of betrayal.

*I*t takes more energy to resist than to be guided by the universal flow.

The learning curve is not a straight line

Be patient with yourself and others.

We see what our brains tell us,
not just what our eyes show us.

Perception is King.
Change your mind's view,
and change your life's course.

→ 36 ←

Smile

It is not the amount of love you
receive that makes the difference. . .

It is the amount of love you
allow yourself to *feel*.

*F*ind your dreams and you will
find your wings.

*T*ruth is uncomplicated.

It is as simple as the sun shining
through a single blade of grass.

*E*mbrace the Ordinary in Extraordinary.

What is extraordinary springs from the simplicity and essence of the ordinary.

*I*s the world a better place
because of the part you play?

*E*ncourage unity that does not
forsake the individual.

$\mathcal{M}$y Father's advice:
"If you have to eat an elephant,
start with the tail."

When confronted with a seemingly
overwhelming project, begin with the
smallest, most manageable part.

A quick success will propel you forward
to tackle the next step,
until the whole task is completed
— piece by successful piece.

*S*ometimes mountains are moved by one
kind act that might only be known
to the recipient.

$\mathcal{Y}$ou are powerful,
and your effect on others is
profound and enduring.

*I*t is easier to say no to the first bite than to the second.

*T*houghts sail along invisible waves and ping with
others resonating at that same frequency. The
harmonic will echo back to you, boosting
and amplifying your original thoughts.

Raise your vibrational frequency
and lift your life.

$\mathcal{T}$he mind leads — the body follows.

⇥ **49** ⇤

*S*poken words don't have a delete key.

*I*t is ok to be "wrong!"

There is no need to defend the indefensible;
no need to spin excuses for
what you feel badly about.

A simple, heartfelt apology allows you to
accept yourself and become more resilient.

Guilt is like a warning flag that appears
to let us know we have done something to
another person that we regret.

We are not meant to stuff it in our
pocket and carry it around.
Rather, the remorseful feeling pops
up to trigger a response.

Acknowlege guilt and confront it head on.

*You can only control your side of the
equation. Once sincerely addressed, if the
other person is not ready to forgive you;
forgive yourself and let it go.*

*Y*our presence is a present.
Come out from your wrappings.

*E*ach day is chock-full of successes.
— No matter how small
— Count them all!

*T*ime taps gently on every back

Reminding all patrons of life's ending track

This host whispers softly to guests in their stay

To seize the moments before time slips away

*E*motions should flow like a river —
They should be
Felt
Experienced
Released

~ 56 ~

*J*udgment is a barrier to truth.

Challenge your assumptions to discern
which belong to you and
which are like ill-fitting clothes
that no longer suit you.

58

$\mathcal{T}$ry Less...

$\mathcal{B}$E More

$\mathcal{M}$istakes are just lessons learned
the hard way.

Courage Comes in Many Colors:

RED   For the courage to recognize and acknowledge anger

YELLOW   For the courage to admit fears and doubts

BLUE   For the courage to speak truth to self and to those in power

ORANGE   For the courage to forgive others for their trespasses

GREEN   For the courage to remain flexible enough to grow and change

PINK   For the courage to feel love with an open heart

PURPLE   For the courage to seek wisdom with an open mind

WHITE   For the courage to arrive at a state of peace, having allowed all the other colors to flow through

*E*mbrace the color wheel of emotions
and find yourself in the flow.

*E*nthusiasm is the engine to joy —
optimism about the future, its fuel.

$\mathcal{L}$earn from the past

$\mathcal{P}$lan for the future

$\mathcal{E}$xperience the present

*W*onder about what you want,
rather than about what you don't want.

Life is not always paved with petals that
lie softly beneath our feet, protecting us
from the harshness of stony paths.

When buffeted by the strong winds
of despair, and the swirling fears
of what might lie ahead. . .

Remember that when you are in the
middle of the worst —
You are already halfway there.

*Y*ou are blessed with wisdom
that glows within you.

*K*eep moving forward, holding onto
your dreams as a guiding light.

If you feel lost in a tempest
or mired in the mud —
Accept your journey.

Change your course.

$\mathcal{H}$ope is desire laced with doubt
　　　Doubt is fear with a sliver of hope

Before a whiff of doubt slips into fear
　　　or calcifies into anger,
Shift your focus to what you want—

　　　Activate a wish—
　　　Fuel a passion—
　　　Imagine and visualize your dream
　　　　like a movie playing before you

Act on it — however small the step

$\mathcal{P}$lanning for the future
with an optimistic outlook
will melt away the barriers to change.

*L*eadership:
The *vision* to see where you are headed;
The *foresight* to see where you would prefer to
          arrive in the future;
The *ability* to craft an effective plan
          to get there;
The *charisma* to inspire others to join you.

The intersection of logic and emotion is:
  — where a line drawing meets its color palette
    — where the skeleton meets its muscle
      — where the mind meets its motion.

*W*e see through a veil of assumptions
that hang on a rod of beliefs.

Challenge your assumptions
Question your beliefs
Reveal your truth

*W*here are you headed?

. . . Is that where you want to be?

You are the conductor
of an invisible orchestra
playing the music of your life.

*Y*our heart holds a compass, and is a beacon
illuminating your destination by
shedding light on the truth.

*E*ach day you walk in the world, you
are a powerful force for change.

We are as connected
as the colors of the rainbow,
and as unique as each color in the rainbow.

Though it is difficult to discern where one
color ends and the other begins, each
glistens with its own hue.

An authentic compliment
is kindness in action.

*H*atred is an abyss.

Holding onto hatred is to lose trust in others and to accept hopelessness.

Leading up to the precipice, you might feel angry, bitter or betrayed…but you only jump off the edge into hatred once you have given up all hope that someone will change.

*L*eap into life.

*B*reach the unknown.

*Y*ou count
And are counted on.

*H*e marched with his boots
Down the path to my heart,
Leaving muddy reminders
Of a mistake from the start.

*D*epression has no bottom floor —

It is like an
elevator
that
continues
to
descend…

until you decide to STOP…
and push the UP button.

That UP button is your will and
determination to focus on something
you want to do, be, or achieve in the future.

$\mathcal{D}$etours might be uncomfortable,
but we can pick up jewels of knowledge
and wisdom along the way
back onto the main highway
of our life's journey.

And for some,
the detour is the journey.

Someone else's confusion doesn't
have to be your misery.

Stay Clear

When conflict arises:
put it all on the table, then
clear the table.

Come prepared with both your
hot knife and the butter.

$\mathcal{B}$etrayed

Shattered mirrors - muddy waters
Reflection's alterations found

Sin dressed up as fragrant flowers
Putrid roots grow underground

False scents inveigle the trusting
Easy prey when unsuspecting

No absolution - no reprieve
From whence the torque of truth deceived

*C*lose the loop of time:

Glean lessons from the past
Engage your senses in the present
Visualize your desired future

"*E*very moment is perfect" —
You just might not like the perfection
of this moment.

$\mathcal{W}$hen in doubt, assume the best.

"When one door closes,
　　　　　another door opens" —

It just might not happen
at the same time.

$\mathscr{N}$egative thoughts slow and lower our vibration
while affirming, optimistic thoughts
ENERGIZE, heal and lift us.

*H*ave the courage to fly in the
face of your fears.

*I*f your dreams remain illusive…

Search for destructive patterns
strung like tripwires in your way —

Convenient excuses to keep
your dreams at bay.

The more we trust in ourselves,
the more the canvas of our future is
painted with optimism and joy.

*I*ntuition is like turning on a radio.

If you hear static, it doesn't mean that your radio "doesn't work." It means that you need to adjust your receiver to tune in.

Once you find your channel, you will be able to receive vast signals.

$\mathcal{D}$read is fear on steroids —
$\mathcal{L}$ove is light unbound.

✦ 99 ✦

*C*uriosity and *A*we
override doubt and resistance.

*W*hen caught in the swirl of
repetitive, negative patterns
—Like a dancer spotting through a turn—
focus on your goals—
move toward your dreams.

When the perfectionist in you creates
roadblocks to completion,
allow yourself to accept that:

Sometimes, good enough is good enough.

Stoke your inner light with self-love.

Through life's mirror,
look past your container
and gaze at your glorious soul.

*F*earless means to Fear—less.

Lower the wall of fear by removing
the magnifying glasses.

*F*ear less . . .

*T*rust more

Rather than seek "company for your misery,"
celebrate others' successes and ignite
your passion and purpose.

*H*umility is a flat open road;
    *A*rrogance is an impediment.

One is a sign of Confidence.
    The other, a sign of Insecurity.

$\mathcal{L}$ike assembling tinker toys, the brain and
emotional system are always seeking and
making connections —

Once made,
they are live wires that send signals
back and forth when triggered by
new experiences.

If you suffer from old, sad connections that
pull your mind into a negative space
and weigh down your heart,
focus on making new connections
that can override those you wish to wither.

The invisible power of wind is no match
for your ability to harness your energy
to generate transformative change.

Nothing is more powerful than
Truth and Love.

High vibration words to meditate on:

Love
Light
Peace
Harmony

A screaming bird in a padded cage
No one to witness the damaging rage

The key is in hand to set yourself free
Fly with open wings toward your destiny

*I*t isn't on any resume when you stopped
using a diaper, bottle, or pacifier.

Move through life at your own pace,
and ignore the blaring sound
of those who put down
arbitrary markers to define your success.

You are the spirit in spiritual.

Life is an adventure — if you get yourself
into the boat.

*D*esire is a magnet toward your dreams.

For those times when it feels like you are
withering in a desert, let your heart's
desire lead you to the oasis.

"*W*hat do you want to be
when you grow up?"

*M*yself

*C*onsider the Source —

Before you follow someone's advice
or accept another's opinion —
Consider the source and let your own
internal wisdom guide you.

*I*n *The Wizard of Oz*,
the "Good Witch" and "Bad Witch" are sisters,
where one wants to empower everyone
and the other wants to exert power
over everyone.

—Which Witch are you?

$\mathcal{L}$ove is a nurturing, supportive force field,
not a teeter totter.
Beware of relationships...

for the other
to be up.

where one needs
to be down

Compete like a swimmer —
in your own lane,
aiming to beat your best time.

Focusing on holding another back
only slows you down anyway.

*Y*our value comes from who you are,
not from what you do.

What you do affects how you experience
life, but is not the measure of your
intrinsic, essential self.

"Comparisons are odious" — Just Be You.

*A*nger is hurt acting out.

*B*eliefs are like seeds and bulbs.
They will grow what you plant.

*A*ccept yourself and others —

*F*orgive yourself and others —

*L*ove yourself and others —

This will allow you to drop burdens,
clear internal clutter, and radiate
from the source of your unique expression.

*W*hen you run away from fear,
your life runs away from you.

Most fears shrink to speed bumps when
you look straight at, instead
of away from, them.

→ 125 ←

Watch your words
— both spoken and silent —
for they are speaking to your heart
and laying the foundation for your future
experiences.

$\mathcal{B}$e aware when the need to "belong" supersedes your courage to stand for what you personally know to be true.

*C*uriosity didn't kill the cat.
It saved its life.

Fascination,
Attention,
Interest,
A desire to Learn,
Investigate,
Discover, and
Glean answers —

All translate into engagement in your
life and the world around you.

$\mathcal{T}$o see is to believe — and
to believe is to see.

$\mathcal{Y}$our honesty is your greatest currency.

*W*hen you are true to yourself,
you will find yourself.

*B*eing and *B*eaming
Show up with your sparkling spirit
and open heart.

$\mathcal{W}$e have

two eyes   one vision.

Focus.

$\mathcal{A}$s you climb the tree of life,
take time to look down and
appreciate how far you have come.

*Y*ou are an original.
You have no duplicate.

*D*econstruct
associations and others' opinions
that form your "Identity" to find yourself.

Rather than "Right vs. Wrong"
— Try "Clear vs. Unclear" —

To engage in a battle of right vs. wrong
is to hold fast in a Tug of War.
Once dug in,
resolution can become illusive.

Search beneath the surface to discover
underlying issues from which
unclarity has taken root.

Ask questions. Then listen and hear.
Look past Ego's roadblocks:
Defending | Deflecting | Denouncing

Like a lamppost shedding light on opposing
roads, this process illuminates the possibility
for reflective dialogue and constructive solutions.

$\mathcal{T}$rue balance does not come from
just resting on the fulcrum,
— that is stasis —
rather, from the ability to embody
opposing qualities simultaneously.

$\mathcal{L}$ike separate water molecules that flow together in the expansive ocean, we are all connected in a swirling energy of humanity — experiencing the ease and tumult together.

When you ease another's pain,
all feel better.
When you raise your vibration,
all are lifted.

*Y*ou are a unique, precious jewel
that is here for a purpose.

Sometimes that purpose feels elusive,
but that doesn't negate the truth of your
importance to the symphony of life.

*T*rying to move forward through grief
can feel like dragging a wet sandbag
tethered to your heart.
Cut the tether

Keep the *L*ove

$\mathcal{F}$ind your $\mathcal{F}$rame

When you say what you feel,
consider their feelings
in how you say it.

Packaged in a clear and conscious frame,
expressed content is received with
greater ease and acceptance.

The easiest way to show unconditional
love is to smile.

$\mathcal{P}$ressure is inevitable.
Our stress reaction is constructive.

Like air in a ball, our stress force
pushes back against outside pressure.

Prolonged or excessive pressure, whether
outside or self inflicted, can wear down,
deflate, and erode our internal force.

What is thought to be "too much stress,"
is in fact…"too much pressure."
Build your stress muscles.
Ease your pressure weights.

*E*ach time we weather the storm,
　　　our roots grow stronger,
　　　our trunk more resilient,
　　　our branches ready to reach farther.

$\mathscr{A}$ betrayal is not a reflection of you.
It is a sign of another's weakness.

$\mathcal{T}$o withhold love
is to diminish your own light.

*T*o rejoice in others' happiness
is to stoke your inner flame.

*I*f you have to scale a mountain,
put on your boots —
but be ready to ride the gondola
when one appears.

Celebrate the high points in life. Creating positive memories will ease your journey through the inevitable low points.

$\mathcal{E}$veryone is $\mathcal{I}$ntuitive

We don't question the power of man-made technology to send invisible messages across a wireless world. So why question the power of brain waves to send and receive messages?

*W*hen fear collides with stress,
it combusts into anxiety.
Delink the fear — Trace it back to its origin
and then release it —
Allowing your internal force to
propel you forward.

What you say and think reveals
what you believe.

*S*peak up:
To muzzle your voice is to stifle
your creative contribution.

"*S*tuck" is an illusion
based on an unclear belief.

Forsake invisible shackles tethered
to that limiting mirage.

We walk through a rainbow of color
every minute of every day.

Just because we don't "see" the colors in
light doesn't mean they aren't there.

What else is beyond our sight?

Universal love and wisdom are like the
sun shining down on all of us.
Some people just choose
to hold an umbrella

which blocks out the beams.

"Apples don't fall far from the tree" —
Unless you were born on a hill.

$\mathcal{F}$or those who don't want to see their
birthday cake melting under a blazing flame
of candles — 3 candles will do —
One for Joy
One for Luck
One for Love

In a relationship, notice if you are like an electron circling around another's nucleus. You are your own atom with an independent and complete orbit and deserve to be with another whole atom, which together form a molecule.

$\mathcal{E}$ach day is an opportunity to
connect or disconnect,
flow or resist.

$\mathcal{A}$llow the ocean of abundance
to flow to you.

Relax — Accept — Receive

Like the soprano whose voice can shatter glass, LOVE is the highest vibration that carries the power to break old patterns, lift your spirit, and allows you to shine with a pure awareness of your innate, inner beauty.

$\mathcal{T}$houghts circle the globe and ultimately
return to you.
Since you will be "hit" with the
same signal you sent,
transmit what you yearn to receive.

$\mathcal{N}$o two voices are alike.
So too with what you have to say.

$\mathcal{P}$ride vs. $\mathcal{E}$go

Pride, in ourselves and what we accomplish,
is an expression of self-love.

Ego forms bricks that build up walls
to protect our perceived
and entrenched identity.

→ 166 ←

$\mathcal{T}$he more we do,
the more we are able to do.

Goals that are set are goals that can
be met — all marathon winners began
with a single, stumbling baby step.

*T*he angels use serendipity, ease, and
resistance to speak with us.

Pay attention . . .
Listen with your life . . .

$\mathcal{F}$ear freezes — $\mathcal{L}$ove flows.

*W*here you aim your vision
is where you direct your life.
Like arrows released from a bow,
you will hit the target you are focused on.

Choose your target wisely.
Aim for the bullseye.

*A*s your life takes flight, be aware that:
DOUBT makes you lose altitude
FEAR stalls the engine

While TRUST is the fuel and force
that propels you forward.

Shame is a dart
Aimed at one's heart
Laced with the poison of self-loathing

With each piercing blow
The proud are brought low
Crushed by Judgment's cruel hammer

*A*ccept what is
Forgive what was
Reflect through eyes of love

$\mathcal{T}$he opposite of curiosity is boredom —
How can a car advance when the engine is
turned off? Turn on your brain's engine
with the key of curiosity.

There is no avoiding life's rollercoaster ride.
So rejoice as you sail through the ups and
relax through the lows, knowing that
as long as you stay strapped in,
a new apex awaits.

Adding "yet" to the end of a hopeless statement shifts present pessimism into a manifest possibility for future success.

"I'm not in a relationship…Yet."
"I'm not in my best shape…Yet."

The power of "Yet" transforms unhelpful, negative programming into a force to magnetize what you desire.

*O*ur 7 Chakras are the same
7 colors of a rainbow.

Let love's light shine through
your full spectrum.

*A*nyone can achieve competence
by putting in the effort —

But a talent is revealed by
what you think is "easy."

Saying "I can't" is to be a victim.

In most cases, it is a substitute for the truth: that you just "don't want to."

Stand empowered by your decisions rather than hiding behind the convenience of "can't."

Millennials, and those born after,
don't have to think out of the box;
they were born out of the box.

*W*ho is driving your bus?
Your emotional limbic brain?
Or your logical frontal cortex?

Together they are the
Map, the Plan, and the Experience.

*W*hen you visualize your dream . . .
charge it with pure intention,
take actions in that direction,
and give it time to manifest.

When baking a cake, you mix the
ingredients, put it in the oven,
and allow it to rise.

Have the same patience with what
you are creating for your future.

*I*f you achieve your goals and dreams and
find yourself still longing and empty,
it is time to reassess your dreams.

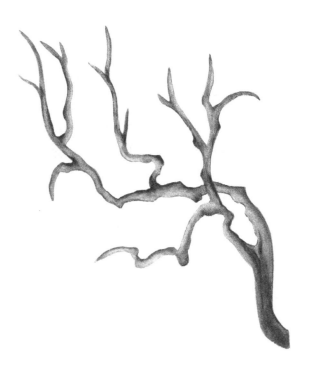

*T*ime is elastic — following a rigid routine
day-after-day, year-after-year
makes time spin faster.

To stretch it like warm taffy:

Change your experiences
Embrace the unknown
Add adventure through exploration
Become enlivened through discovery
Choose to be uncomfortable

. . . which in time, will transform into
new areas of comfort.

*T*hrough opaque lenses
He cannot see the brightness
That shines around him

*S*ee with your mind
Listen with your discernment
Dream with your heart
Trust with your soul
Act with your passionate spirit
Feel as you breathe

Create a partnership between your mind,
soul, and heart and your path will be
brightly lit and your way ahead clear.

Boxes are for objects not for people.

*W*hat you say to yourself is like
the ocean's undertow.
What others say to you is like the waves.
While you can't control the weather and the
waves, you can, and do, control the undertow.

*E*veryone is gifted — just at what?

Brush aside the debris of doubt
and discover your gifts.

A dream that is suppressed is a
flower that never blooms.

*E*mpower Yourself.
*C*laim your Destiny.

*Y*ou are precious.

— Stay away from those who seek to smash your inner crystal and snuff your inner light.

*Y*ou are surrounded by
universal love and support

— Feel the embrace.

The force of your will is fueled by your passion—Your passion flows from a sense of purpose—Your purpose is illuminated by your talents.

*A*dd up your wins —
rather than your losses.

Allow your vivid imagination
to raise you above your fears and
let your dreams take flight.

$\mathcal{F}$ears are like fires signaling what
we are here to work on.

$\mathcal{F}$ears' flames are fanned when ignored
and snuffed out when confronted.

*B*eing right is not a destination.

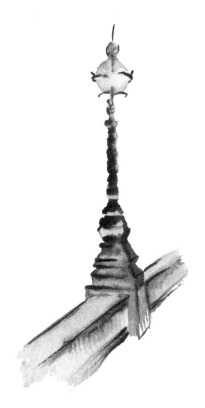

*B*eliefs trigger thoughts . . .
Thoughts direct choices . . .
Choices lead to action or inaction . . .
Which determine how you will experience life.

*Y*ou are performing a script
inspired by your beliefs,
written by your thoughts,
with a cast chosen by you,
performed for an audience
you have gathered.

Ready — "I am ready. . ."

A powerful phrase to leap over resistance and help you to attract your desired dreams and goals.

To question your worthiness to give and
receive love betrays your very essence.
An infant barely moves, yet soaks up
love and attention.

You are still that newborn,
wise and worthy of unconditional love.

*B*etter to unleash your creativity
than to cloak who you are
just to fit in.

The story of Adam and Eve
is the first communication breakdown
between a man and woman.

Rather than tell Eve the truth, Adam
instead chose to control Eve's behavior by
embellishing upon G-d's directive not to eat
from the Tree of Knowledge, claiming that
even touching the tree would have
catastrophic consequences.

The Snake easily exposed this lie, which
unraveled the trust Eve placed on Adam's
word and led to the ultimate breach.

It still holds true that:
Without truth, there is no trust. Without trust,
a relationship has a fractured foundation.

$\mathcal{B}$abies are born curious about
everything — keep your curiosity alive and
experience the wonder in wonderful.

*T*eaching the "older generation" how to use
technology is like standing on land
while explaining how to swim to
someone who has never seen
or experienced water.

Patience!

Criticism doesn't have to be critical.

Confidence is a state of being.
Courage is the ability to act regardless
of outside pressures.

*I*f you feel like an orchid
blooming alone in the desert…

*M*ove.

*F*eeling jealous of another means you doubt your ability to create your dreams.

*T*o know you is to love you.

"*W*herever you go, you take yourself with you."

But there will be new mirrors
and new reflections —

And the possibility for new awareness.

Wisdom's light can't penetrate the walls of delusion.

When one's ego insists on seeing oneself
in the "right" through eyes that
refuse to look inward…

See(k) in-sight

*R*esponsibilities should be shouldered.
— Credit shared —

*W*hat is possible?

You tell yourself everyday by
what you think and what you do

*W*hat is success?

Each step taken in the direction
of your goals and dreams

Opinions are like air in a balloon
that can pop and disappear
whereas

Truth is absolute
- immutable
- a platform for wisdom
Facts are concrete blocks

Build on Facts | Pursue Wisdom

Rather than idle at the crossroads of indecision;
Or drive in reverse — afraid to face the unkown

Find your way forward —

Think . . .

Feel . . .

Do . . .

𝒯he "I" in Identity starts with You.

Setting standards of perfection as unrealistic guides by which to judge yourself diminishes your unique presence and purpose.

$\mathcal{W}$hen someone tries to lead you across
their bridge, be sure that
it isn't "the plank."

*W*here is that "Dull Moment?"

*O*ur time here is like an open suitcase that
gets filled with our experiences. As
the horizon approaches, and we
close the case, it is easy to say,
"Where did all the time go?"

*B*ut the measure of our time
is in the weight of what we packed.

*B*e above

*F*ly above

*R*ise above

Self-worth is a Misnomer

There is no gauge or measure or estimate
that determines the "value" of you!
You are priceless – sui generis

See Yourself — Know Yourself
Be Yourself

$\mathcal{G}$-d doesn't make mistakes.
You are here for a reason.
Rejoice in the glory of you.

$\mathcal{A}$t the end — all that really matters is:

The love we feel,
The connections we make, and
The experiences we have.

*M*ay you experience your current dreams as your future reality.

Living a full life means facing
Moments that can feel as:

Chilling *and* **Bitter...**

as an arctic tundra...

Painful...

as a soldier wounded in battle...

Uncertain...

as walking through a twisting maze...

Lonely...

as a single owl hooting into the still night...

Challenging...

as navigating a ship through a blustering tempest...

Anxious...

as feeling lost in a dark forest without a flashlight,
match or compass...

Therefore...

Living Large is not for the faint of heart.

*It requires a fierce determination, resilience,
trust, optimism, and the ability to move
forward in the face of raging doubts
and withering fears.*

*Each day that you marshal your resources
to manage the moment,
you prove your courage and grit.*

What a Champion You Are!